LOVE AND RAIN

Poems of the Way

by

BARRY GRAHAM

DOCKYARD PRESS

ISBN 978-1-913452-44-5

for Daishin Stephenson:

thirty-six years,
thirty-six bows

LOVE AND RAIN

stainless steel table cold to touch
pale skin of leg
hair growing from skin

night birds, starlight, desert wind —
moth wings beat
against computer screen

summer evening —
man in motorized wheelchair
walks his poodle

the hours of contemplation —
thoughts, exhausted, fall
to the floor of the mind

the dog behind the fence
barks at the man walking by —
but his tail is wagging

winter desert city —
icy sunshine
melts into night

the broken wall
of the old slaughterhouse
can't keep out the rain

sunset—
the cat drinking
from the pond

first autumn moon —
by its light
I see my breath

snow falls
on the cardinal
sitting on a bare branch

cold sunlight
between tree branches —
January Sunday

sunbeam on
counter,
cast-iron teakettle

wind chimes, empty porch swing rocks —
the wild cat I feed
has not been seen for days

nothing old, nothing new —
every year the moon
and the frost

the winter moon —
a jewel
for her nakedness

afternoon rain —
two naked bodies
asleep in tangled sheets

night kitchen warmed
by cast-iron skillet
glowing red-hot on stove

November morning fog —
bare branches,
cold windows

watching sun rise
over empty streets —
the end of summer

brushing stray cat,
pulling burrs
from his coat

after midnight —
tears on my face,
moon over the city

Afternoon storm, rain thick as fog —
thunder explodes, the woods tremble —
in the shelter of a porch,
a feral cat
sleeps through it all.

The thunder stops,
the storm is over —
rain drips from the gutters,
and a sleeping cat
wakes, stretches, yawns.

A firefly gets inside the house —
one swipe of a cat's paw, and it falls.
It lies there on the wood floor,
its light still blinking, the
dark moments growing longer and longer.

I wish I could be your armor,
stand in front of you
or wrap myself around you, blocking
all that has hurt you
and all that will hurt you.

A winter day in August —
cold shock as I get out of bed —
fish in the pond too sluggish to feed,
cat lies on gazebo
in shaft of icy sunlight.

Email brings bad news of a friend.
The last time I saw him, we sang songs together —voices
colliding, then blending. Now his voice
is a lonely whisper, and I sing a song of sadness
on a moonless night.

A greasy diner in a southern town,
night — a man sits in a booth, reads
a newspaper, drinks iced tea. A woman
walks in, looks for him. His face erupts
in a smile as he stands up and waves.

Rain falling on this house
by the woods —
the same rain that falls
on the hospital
where she sleeps tonight.

Full moon shines
on your desert and
my forest,
your street and
my garden.

Freezing —
full moon hangs low
over the factories
and a dog barks
from midnight until dawn.

Winter sunlight
through the kitchen window —
cat on the dining table
raises his sleepy head,
looks at me, and I laugh.

December morning. Rain.
You are not here,
but with every note of music
and every sip of tea
you are in my arms.

Day cold, apartment warm,
cocooned by music and rain —
purring cat rolls around on the couch
and I am so happy
I laugh and cry at the same time.

After days of spring weather,
winter has returned —
snow is falling
and I am kept warm
by thoughts of you.

The wind through the forest
roars like an ocean —
snow blows across my porch,
toppling furniture
and slamming the door.

Bird feeder swinging
back and forth
in the wind and the snow —
little bird hangs on,
eating, eating, eating.

Morning after ice storm —
pour hot coffee in cold cup,
check that the wild birds
have enough to eat,
bow to the Buddha.

Lying on the porch swing
in afternoon breeze,
I close the book I've been reading
and look at the sky
as a frog barks at the pond.

Kansas City Airport,
one week from Christmas —
California girl
talks on her cell phone —
blonde hair, college sweatshirt

Two small birds
building a nest on
my porch —
flying back and forth,
working together.

The birds have mated,
built nests together
in the sun —
do they know
how quickly it passes?

Food on the plate,
tea in the cup —
say your thanks.
Say it to the sunlight,
say it to the rain.

Spring night —
I walk outside
to take a piss
and warm rain
falls on me.

On the porch,
I chant a sutra.
By the pond,
a frog barks.
Between us, the rain.

Gloaming. Rain falls
on the pond
as the fish rise
to the food
I have brought them.

Tadpoles dancing
in dark water
between feeding fish —
above them, the
first fireflies of the year

June, early morning
darkness — in my yard,
lightning and rain
on my naked body
as I remember her.

Fading daylight —
deer feeds in
my yard while
fireflies dance
around her.

Just the wind
shaking the trees
outside my house
on a cloudy Saturday
October morning.

Fierce blue sky,
ground white with frost —
roosters screeching
through the cold
Saturday morning.

Driving in the cold,
he can see his breath.
He remembers the heat
of her body. Her taste
is still in his mouth.

Less than thirty degrees tonight.
Huddled in layers of clothes,
I drink tea and read.
A stew simmers on the stove,
and I wish you were here.

My house sits
on the edge of woods,
a half-mile from a mental hospital —
some nights, I hear
the screech of alarms.

The road ends
at the hospital,
but traffic is brisk —
people who work there,
people who visit.

Rain leaks
through the chimney,
making a pool around
the Buddha statue
in the fireplace.

One in the morning,
I'm startled by
a light at the window —
a firefly.
I greet it like an old friend.

Cleaning the cats'
litter box, I bow
to clumps of piss and shit
and the creatures
who watch me serve them.

Alone, he remembers
an unfamiliar room,
tangled sheets, open window,
her cheek on his thigh.
"You taste like rain," she said.

A Zen monk
must wake very early
in order to have time to jerk off
before the bell rings
for morning meditation.

Even if I believed in gods,
I would still prefer Buddhas.
Omnipotence is easy —
living, loving, cleaning the toilet
are acts of magic.

September evening —
the sun turns red,
and crickets drown out
the sound of cars
as I ride my bicycle.

She talks on the phone
to her cousin
while I knead pieces
of ground deer-flesh
into the shape of burgers.

Dark and stinging cold outside.
A cat walks slowly through
the complex, head down.
In my apartment, vegetable soup
simmers on the stove.

Cat asleep
on floor
under strobing fan
using Dogen's *Shobogenzo*
for her pillow.

In her dreams
she is falling.
When she wakes,
gasping, his arms
are around her.

I chant, burning incense
in Phoenix, Arizona.
A friend hears it,
breathes in the smoke
in Okayama, Japan.

Stretched out on the couch
with her, drinking plum wine,
reading *The Diamond Sutra* aloud —
all of birth, life and death
contained in her smile.

He says someone hit him
with some pipe. Through the blood,
you can see the white of his skull.
He doesn't want an ambulance,
but asks for a dollar.

Food, tea,
time with friends,
a dying cat —
sunlight each day,
darkness each night.

The monastery cook
was chanting the *Tenzo Kyokun*
when a splash of water from the pan
burned the sight from his eye.
No one knows, ever.

In the convenience store
a woman counts change,
a penny at a time,
to buy a single can
of malt liquor.

Kneeling on the back seat,
hanging out of the window,
vomiting into the desert night
with a pornographer at the wheel
and the birthday girl riding shotgun

Who's right? Who's wrong?
Who's good? Who's bad?
The answer is written
on every gravestone
in every cemetery

ABOUT THE AUTHOR

Barry Graham is what Foucault called an Author Function.